J
294.6
GAN

Ganeri, Anita, 1961-

The milk and the
jasmine flower and
other stories

CANCELLED
MAY 05 2008

D1171620

Stories from Faiths
Sikhism

The Milk and the Jasmine Flower

and Other Stories

QEB

Copyright © 2007 QEB Publishing

First published in the United States by
QEB Publishing, Inc.
23062 La Cadena Drive
Laguna Hills, CA 92653

www.qeb-publishing.com

All rights reserved. No part of this publication may be reproduced,
stored in a retrieval system, or transmitted in any form or by any means,
electronic, mechanical, photocopying, recording, or otherwise, without
the prior permission of the publisher, nor be otherwise circulated in any
form of binding or cover other than that in which it is published and
without a similar condition being imposed on the subsequent purchaser.

Library of Congress Control Number: 2007001013

ISBN 978 1 59566 379 5

Written by Anita Ganeri
Design and editorial by East River Partnership
Illustrated by Olwyn Whelan
Series Consultant Roger Butler

Publisher Steve Evans
Creative Director Zeta Davies
Senior Editor Hannah Ray

Printed and bound in China

Stories from Faiths
Sikhism

The Milk and the
Jasmine Flower

and Other Stories

Anita Ganeri

Illustrated by Olwyn Whelan

QEB

The Rich Man and the Needle

Long ago, there was a rich man named Duni Chand. He lived in a very grand house with seven flags flying from the roof.

One day, the great Sikh teacher
Guru Nanak visited the city
where Duni Chand lived. Duni
Chand was very excited and
invited Guru Nanak to his house.

Guru Nanak asked Duni Chand why he had flags flying from his roof. Proudly, Duni Chand told him that the flags showed everyone how rich he was.

Duni Chand then said to Guru Nanak that, although he was a rich man, he was not happy. Duni Chand told Guru Nanak that he wanted to be the richest man in the whole city.

Smiling, Guru Nanak gave
Duni Chand a precious silver
needle. Guru Nanak told him
to look after it and to give it
back to him in the next world.

When Duni Chand showed the needle to his wife, she laughed and told him not to be so silly. He could not take a needle with him when he died!

Guru Nanak told Duni Chand that his wife was right. He would have to leave the needle behind, and all his gold and riches as well.

Duni Chand felt ashamed that he had been so greedy. And, from that day, he promised to use his money and riches to help the poor.

The Milk and the Jasmine Flower

One day, Guru Nanak and his friend Mardana came to the city of Multan. They had been traveling for many days and were tired and hungry.

Many holy men lived
in Multan. People gave
them money for their
advice and wise words.
But, over time, the holy
men had become
rich and greedy.

The holy men did not want Guru Nanak in their city. They thought that he would spoil everything because people loved him more than them. So they came up with a plan to make Guru Nanak leave Multan.

The holy men sent a large bowl
of milk to Guru Nanak. The bowl
was so full that there was not
room for a single drop more.

By giving him the full bowl of milk, the holy men were showing Guru Nanak that their city was already full of holy men.

When Guru Nanak saw the milk, he picked a jasmine flower and dropped it into the bowl. The delicate flower was so light that it floated without spilling a single drop of milk.

Guru Nanak wanted to show the holy men that there is always room for more holiness in the world. Just as there was room for the flower in the bowl of milk.

When they saw what Guru Nanak had done
with the flower, the holy men were sorry that
they had been rude. So, they gave Guru Nanak
and Mardana a warm welcome to their city.

The Princes and the Guru's Cloak

Long ago, an emperor named Jahangir was riding in the forest when a tiger attacked him. Luckily, Guru Hargobind was passing by and saved the emperor's life. The two men then became good friends.

One day, the emperor became ill. He
called for his friend Guru Hargobind.
Jahangir asked the Guru to go to a nearby
fort and pray for him until he got better.

Guru Hargobind agreed to go to the fort. But, when he arrived there, he found that he was not alone. Fifty-two poor princes were being kept prisoner in the fort.

Guru Hargobind felt sorry for the princes, all of whom wore dirty clothes and looked very hungry. He wanted to help them, so he gave them some of his food.

When the emperor felt well again, he sent a message to tell Guru Hargobind that he could leave the fort. But, Guru Hargobind did not want to leave.

Guru Hargobind told the emperor
that he would only leave the fort on
one condition. The emperor must allow
the fifty-two princes to leave with him.

The emperor did not want to allow all of the princes to go free. He told Guru Hargobind that he could take with him only those princes who could hold onto his cloak.

So, Guru Hargobind made a cloak with fifty-two tassels, one for each prince to hold. Then, he walked out of the fort with all of the fifty-two princes behind him!

The Guru and the Holy Bread

There was once an old lady who was very holy. She was teased by the other villagers because she often prayed that the great Sikh teacher, Guru Har Rai, would eat her homemade bread.

Although the old lady was poor, she saved some money to buy a big bag of flour. Then she baked two tasty loaves of bread with the flour.

The old lady set off with the bread
to a place that she knew Guru Har Rai
was likely to pass. When she arrived
there, she sat down and waited.

Sure enough, the Guru soon appeared. He had been riding in the nearby forest with his followers. He was now tired and very hungry.

Guru Har Rai saw the old lady and climbed down from his horse. She was overjoyed and could not believe her eyes. Her prayers were about to be answered.

When the old lady offered Guru Har Rai some of her homemade bread, he took it and ate it gratefully. After finishing his meal, he thanked her and rode away.

Later that day, the Guru's followers
made him some special cakes to eat.
When the Guru did not eat them, his
followers asked him what was wrong.

The Guru told them that the old lady's simple bread was the most delicious he had ever tasted. And that was because she had made it with great love and holiness.

Notes for Parents and Teachers

About Sikhism

Sikhism began in the Punjab region of northwest India about 500 years ago. At that time, the two major religions in India were Hinduism and Islam, but there were many conflicts between the two. Nanak (1469–1539), a holy man, introduced the new religion, which taught tolerance and equality for all. He became the first of ten Sikh holy teachers, called Gurus. After the death of the tenth Guru, the Sikhs' holy book, the Guru Granth Sahib, became the Sikhs' guide. Sikhs believe in one God, and the purpose of a Sikh's life is to grow closer to God. They hope to do this by remembering God in everything they say or do. They also try to live honest lives and care for others without thought of their own reward.

About the stories in this book

In each of the world's religions, stories play an essential part. For centuries, they have been used to teach people about the traditions and beliefs of their religion in an accessible way, making difficult ideas and concepts easier to understand. For children in today's multicultural society, these stories also provide an ideal introduction to the different faiths, their key figures, and beliefs.

The Rich Man and the Needle

This is one of the many stories told about Guru Nanak, who spent much of his life traveling around India teaching people about God. Each story about his travels has an important message. In "The Rich Man and the Needle," Guru Nanak teaches Duni Chand that the most important things in life are not gold and riches, but living a holy life and helping others. What good will all of Duni Chand's riches do him if he cannot even take a simple needle with him when he dies?

The Milk and the Jasmine Flower

When Guru Nanak went on his travels, he often took a friend named Mardana with him. Mardana was a musician and a Muslim. He and Guru Nanak grew up in the same village and had been friends since childhood. Guru Nanak had himself been brought up as a Hindu, and had many Hindu and Muslim friends. A key teaching of Sikhism is respect and acceptance of other people and their views. The story also illustrates Guru Nanak's teaching that there is always room for more goodness, kindness, and holiness in the world.

The Princes and the Guru's Cloak

The story of "The Princes and the Guru's Cloak" is the story behind the Sikh festival of Bandi Chhorh Divas, which occurs on the same day as Diwali and is celebrated in October or November. (Diwali, one of the most important Hindu festivals, is now an almost universal Indian festival.) At the time of Diwali, Sikhs remember Guru Hargobind's release from prison and his return to the city of Amritsar. The Sikhs decorated the Harimandir (Golden Temple) with lights to welcome him home. Today, Sikhs light their homes with lamps, set off fireworks, and illuminate the Harimandir in Amritsar once more.

The Guru and the Holy Bread

The theme of this story is that actions that are performed with sincerity and genuine love are always rewarded by God. The old lady in the story is mocked by her fellow villagers because she dares to think that Guru Har Rai may be interested in her humble bread. But, because it is made with great love and devotion, the Guru is touched and stops to eat it. In fact, sharing food is extremely important in Sikhism, in order to show that everyone is equal. In the Sikh practice of Langar, free vegetarian food is served in the Gurdwara—the Sikh temple—and is intended to be eaten by all as equals.

Further things to do

• Read the stories aloud to the children. Talk about the stories with them. Ask them questions about what they think the stories mean. For example, why did Guru Har Rai eat the old lady's bread? How did the old lady feel about that?

• Relate the stories to experiences in the children's own lives. For example, talk about Guru Hargobind helping the princes. Have they ever helped anyone? Think about the Guru's friends and about the children's own friends, and how important it is to listen to them.

• Use a variety of different ways to tell the stories. The children could act out the stories, making masks and costumes for their characters to wear. Music plays an important part in Sikh worship, so you could source some Punjabi music and set the plays to it.

• Find out more about the Harimandir in Amritsar, India, which is the Sikhs' most sacred site. Extend this activity to investigate other Sikh festivals and the stories behind them.